Katydids
Leaf Look-alikes

DISAPPEARING ACTS

by Natalie Lunis

Consultant: Brian V. Brown
Curator, Entomology Section
Natural History Museum of Los Angeles County

BEARPORT
PUBLISHING

NEW YORK, NEW YORK

Credits

Cover, © Morley Read/Alamy and Amazon Images MBSI/Alamy; TOC, © Dave Brenner/iStockphoto; 4-5, © Michael Fogden/DRK Photo; 6T, © Mark Bowler/NHPA/Photoshot; 6B, © Pete Oxford/Nature Picture Library; 7, © Piotr Naskrecki/Minden Pictures; 8, © Bernard Photo Productions/Animals Animals Enterprises; 9, © Pete Oxford/Minden Pictures; 10, © George Grall/NGS Image Collection; 11, © Satoshi Kuribayashi/Nature Production/Minden Pictures; 13, © André Skonieczny/Photolibrary; 14, © George Bernard/NHPA/Photoshot; 15, © Pete Oxford/Minden Pictures; 17, © Derrick Alderman/Alamy; 18T, © F1online digitale Bildagentur GmbH/Alamy; 18B, © Piotr Naskrecki/Minden Pictures; 19, © Richard Shiell/Animals Animals Enterprises; 21, © Pete Oxford/Minden Pictures; 22L, © B. Mete Uz/Alamy; 22C, © Dwight Kuhn Photography; 22R, © James Carmichael Jr./NHPA/Photoshot; 23TL, © Jennifer Foeller/iStockphoto; 23TR, © iStockphoto; 23ML, © macro lens/Shutterstock; 23MR, © orionmystery/Shutterstock; 23BL, © Stana/Shutterstock; 23BR, © Ra'id Khalil/Shutterstock.

Publisher: Kenn Goin
Editorial Director: Adam Siegel
Creative Director: Spencer Brinker
Design: Kim Jones
Photo Researcher: Picture Perfect Professionals, LLC

Library of Congress Cataloging-in-Publication Data

Lunis, Natalie.
  Katydids : leaf look-alikes / by Natalie Lunis.
     p. cm. — (Disappearing acts)
  Includes bibliographical references and index.
  ISBN-13: 978-1-936087-40-2 (library binding)
  ISBN-10: 1-936087-40-5 (library binding)
  1. Katydids—Juvenile literature. 2. Camouflage (Biology)—Juvenile literature. I. Title.
  QL508.T4L86 2010
  595.7'26—dc22
                              2009030786

For more information, write to Bearport Publishing Company, Inc., 101 Fifth Avenue, Suite 6R, New York, New York 10003. Printed in the United States of America in North Mankato, Minnesota.

112009
090309CGC

10 9 8 7 6 5 4 3 2 1

Contents

Keep Looking

It's a breezy day in a green, leafy forest.

Twigs and leaves sway gently in the wind.

Look very closely, however.

One of those leaves isn't a leaf at all.

It's a **grasshopper** called a katydid!

Leaves with Legs

There are thousands of different kinds of katydids.

Yet most of these grasshoppers don't hop in the grass.

Instead, they live, hop, and hide among leaves.

Some live among green leaves, and some live among dead brown leaves.

They disappear from sight by looking just like the plant life around them.

katydid

katydid

Katydids live all over the world. They are found just about everywhere that plants grow. However, most kinds live in warm, wet forests.

Staying Out of Sight, Staying Alive

Many animals, including birds, spiders, snakes, and lizards called geckos, like to eat katydids.

The grasshoppers are often able to hide from their enemies, however, by blending in with the leaves around them.

Hungry animals usually pass right by the katydids, missing out on a tasty treat.

katydid

gecko

Not all katydids look like leaves. Some look like tree bark. Some look like **moss**.

9

Hidden by Darkness

Most kinds of katydids stay still during the day.

The only time they move is when they sway like leaves in the wind.

When night comes and they are hidden by darkness, they start to move around and look for food.

Most kinds of katydids eat leaves and other plant parts. Some kinds, however, eat other **insects**.

Flying Leaps

Even though katydids are well hidden, enemies sometimes find them.

Luckily, katydids are built to make a quick escape.

First they use their long, powerful back legs to take off with a big jump.

Then they open their wings and fly.

Like all grasshoppers, katydids have two pairs of wings. The outer pair is usually leaf-shaped. It covers and protects a thin, clear inner pair.

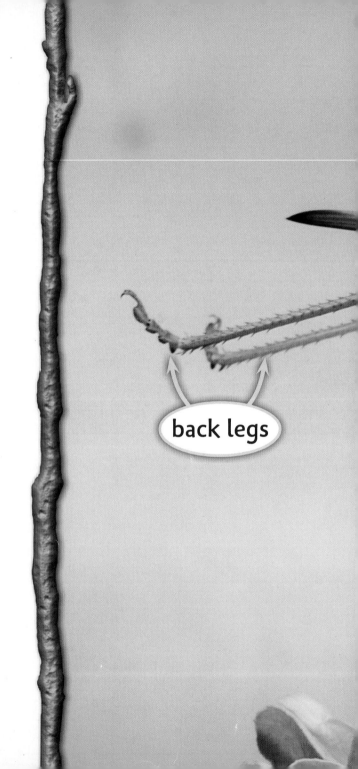

back legs

inner wings

outer wings

Wings That Sing

Katydids use their wings for more than flying.

Males rub their outer wings together to make music.

They play their songs to attract females so they can mate with them.

Both male and female katydids have a pair of large ears for hearing songs and other sounds. The ears are not on their heads, however. They are on their front legs.

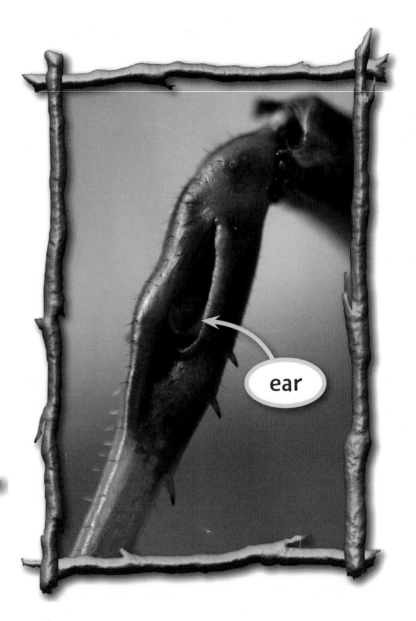

ear

ear

ear

A Musical Name

Each kind of katydid chirps a different song.

One kind, however, has a song that gave this large group of grasshoppers its name.

It is sometimes called the "true katydid."

When it played its song, people thought they heard the words *"Katy-did, Katy-did."*

Where True Katydids Live

The true katydid lives in most parts of the eastern and central United States.

Hatching in Spring

In places with cold winters, female katydids lay their eggs in the fall.

When the cold weather comes, the adult katydids do not survive, but the eggs do.

Baby katydids hatch from them in the spring.

Like all baby grasshoppers, they are called **nymphs**.

In forests that are warm year-round, katydids lay their eggs at different times during the year.

katydid laying eggs

eggs

nymphs

Disappearing from View

At first, katydid nymphs do not have wings.

Then, as their bodies get bigger and bigger, their leaf-like wings start to grow.

Soon the fully grown katydids seem to disappear into their surroundings.

They can easily be heard, however, when they start to fill the air with their loud, clear songs.

In addition to *"Katy-did, Katy-did,"* the musical grasshoppers make sounds like *"chip, chip,"* *"tick, tick, tick, tick,"* and *"zip, zip, zip, zee-ee-ee."*

More Disappearing Acts

Katydids aren't the only creatures that hide by looking just like the plant life around them. Here are three more insects that are camouflaged to look like plant parts.

Walkingstick

Orchid Mantis

Thorn Bug

Glossary

camouflage
(KAM-uh-flahzh)
colors and markings on
an animal's body that
help it blend in with
its surroundings

grasshopper
(GRASS-*hop*-ur) an
insect that has long,
powerful back legs
and can jump far

insects (IN-sekts)
small animals that have
six legs, three body
parts, two antennas,
and a hard covering
called an exoskeleton

moss (MAWSS)
a fuzzy green plant
that sometimes
covers rocks or tree
bark

nymphs (NIMFS)
baby grasshoppers

Index

Read More

Bishop, Nic. *Katydids.* Katonah, NY: Richard C. Owen (1998).

Cooper, Jason. *Katydids.* Vero Beach, FL: Rourke (2006).

Goldish, Meish. *Leaping Grasshoppers.* New York: Bearport Publishing (2008).

Learn More Online

To learn more about katydids, visit
www.bearportpublishing.com/DisappearingActs

About the Author

Natalie Lunis has written many science and nature books for children. She hides out among the leaves and trees in the Hudson River Valley, just north of New York City.